CHILDREN'S AND PARENTS' SERVICES
PATCHOGUE-MEDFORD LIBRARY

If you have a home computer with Internet access you may:

- request an item to be placed on hold.
- renew an item that is not overdue or on hold.
- view titles and due dates checked out on your card.
- view and/or pay your outstanding fines online (over $5).

To view your patron record from your home computer click on
Patchogue-Medford Library's homepage: **www.pmlib.org**

MAKING ART WITH PAPER

Gillian Chapman & Pam Robson

PowerKiDS
press.
New York

All projects should be done carefully, with an adult's help and supervision wh
appropriate (especially for activities involving any cutting, carving, or sewing
An adult should execute or supervise any work with a craft knife, and safe
scissors should be used for all cutting.

Published in 2008 by The Rosen Publishing Group, Inc.
29 East 21st Street, New York, NY 10010

First Edition

Library of Congress Cataloging-in-Publication Data

Chapman, Gillian.
  Making art with paper / Gillian Chapman & Pam Robson. -- 1st ed.
       p. cm. -- (Everyday art)
  Includes index.
  ISBN-13: 978-1-4042-3725-4 (library binding)
  ISBN-10: 1-4042-3725-9 (library binding)
  1. Paper work--Juvenile literature. 2. Waste paper--Recycling--Juvenile
literature. I. Robson, Pam. II. Title.
  TT870.C454 2007
  745.54--dc22

                                                2006028552

Manufactured in China

Contents

Paper from Fibers

Paper is made from fibrous natural materials like wood or cotton. The Chinese made paper from fibers of flax and grass. The ancient Egyptians used papyrus stems; the word *paper* is derived from the word *papyrus*. In Bangladesh today, paper is made from waste jute and water hyacinths.

Most of our paper is made from wood. Wood is firm because it contains lignin in its cell walls. Lignin causes white paper to turn yellow when it is exposed to sunlight. Old newspapers develop an extremely yellowed appearance.

Creating Art from Paper

Developing countries have led the world in the use of found materials for craftwork. At first, this was because of poverty and lack of resources, but today there is a worldwide demand for such works of art. Often the original product names are still visible on the finished artifacts.

Papier-mâché plate made at Srinigar, in the Indian province of Kashmir.

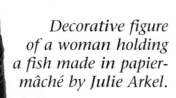

Decorative figure of a woman holding a fish made in papier-mâché by Julie Arkel.

In Haiti, cement bags are recycled and turned into papier-mâché from which beautiful decorated models are created. In Thailand, newspaper is recycled by craftspeople. Miniature baskets are made from newspaper strips wound around wire. Scraps of mulberry paper left over by kite makers are used to make boxes. Peruvian women make rolled paper necklaces out of coiled strips of paper cut from magazines — the strips are barely .04 in (1 mm) wide.

Trees

Reusing paper and cardboard helps to save our forests and woodlands, and it also conserves energy. Most paper is made from softwood trees, like spruce, which grow faster than hardwoods. However, fast-growing softwood plantations are unsuitable as habitats for important ecosystems. Many plants and animals need mixed woodland and forests to survive.

Recycled Paper

Today, many everyday paper products are made from recycled paper. This book suggests useful ways to reuse paper and cardboard. We should recycle paper products, not only to save our trees, but also to reduce the mountains of waste collecting on the Earth. Many towns now have collection points for recyclable items like paper, aluminum cans, and glass.

The Lone Star Cowboy by Philip Cox, 1993 — a life-size papier-mâché sculpture.

Newspaper packed up and ready for recycling in Andorra.

Always sort garbage, only throwing away those things that cannot be recycled. A lot of the waste that is thrown into garbage cans is deposited in landfill sites where dangerous gases can build up. Sometimes these gases are used to produce energy. Waste is also disposed of by incineration or burning — but this causes toxic fumes to collect in the atmosphere. We live in a fast-moving, disposable society. The Earth's natural resources are limited. If we make smart use of our garbage, those resources will last much longer.

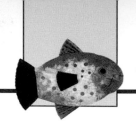

Patterns in Paper

Collecting Waste Papers

Many people think of waste paper as garbage, but it has many uses. It also has some amazing qualities. Paper can be rough, tough, delicate, smooth, translucent, opaque, light, or heavy. Waste printed papers can be colorful, interesting, and are mostly free.

Start to make a paper collection now, and see how many types of paper you can find. Collect labels, tickets, cards, paper wrappers, envelopes, old sheets of music and maps, magazines and newspapers, junk mail, giftwrap, catalogues, and brochures. Look for a range of colors and thicknesses. Not all scrap paper will be suitable for project work.

Sorting and Storing Paper

Each of the projects in this book requires a different kind of paper. Plain papers can be sorted according to their properties. Strong brown paper will need to be separated from delicate tissue paper. Printed papers can be sorted into colors, patterns, pictures, or words. Organize your paper into different categories. Gummed or waxed paper cannot be recycled, so reuse envelopes if possible.

Keep paper away from direct sunlight, especially newspaper. Large pieces of paper are best stored flat. Smaller items, like old postcards, tickets, and greeting cards, can be kept in boxes.

Collection of Different Scrap Papers

Tearing Paper

Paper can be torn, cut, and twisted into many forms. Its properties can be altered by folding and rolling. You can change the look and feel of the paper, and make it stronger.

All paper is much easier to tear along the grain. To test for the grain direction, first tear across the sheet and then from top to bottom and notice the difference. Tearing paper along the edge of a ruler gives a neater finish.

Folding and Rolling

Thin paper will fold neatly, but thicker paper or cardboard will need to be scored first with a blunt knife. Practice folding pieces of paper of different thicknesses, making the folds as sharp as possible.

Make paper curls to decorate your models by wrapping long strips of paper tightly around a pencil. It is easier to roll paper into a tube or cylinder by rolling with the grain. This will make a tighter tube.

Pleating and Cutting

Make a series of small folds or pleats in a strip of paper. Fans of pleated papers can be used to decorate models.

Cutting simple patterns into paper with a craft knife can produce interesting textures, but only do this when you have an adult to help.

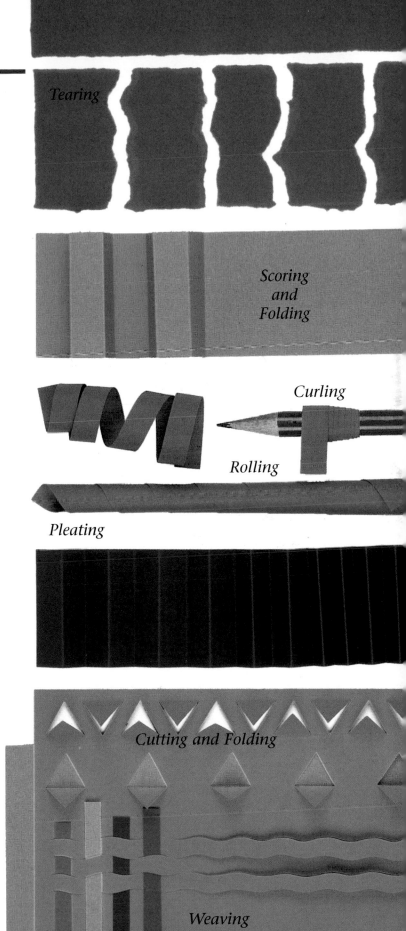

Tearing

Scoring and Folding

Curling

Rolling

Pleating

Cutting and Folding

Weaving

7

Paper Collage

Artists at Work

Many artists use found materials in their work. Both Matisse and Schwitters used different forms of scrap paper and printed material in their collages. The British artist, Philip Cox, began using cardboard and waste paper to make his life-size figures, because he could not afford to buy art materials.

Envelope Collages

Envelopes are ideal materials to use for an environmentally friendly collage. They cannot be recycled because of the gum. Collect envelopes of different shapes and colors to make your collage. Show the address side and the stamps if they are interesting, or have the flap open and tuck papers and messages inside.

Envelope Collage

Lettering Collage

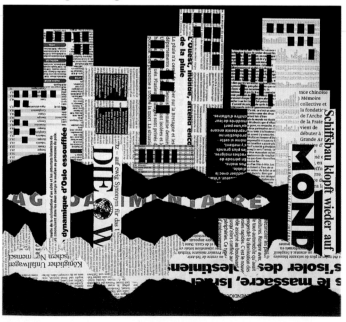

Lettering

In newspapers and magazines, we see lettering in a range of styles and sizes. Create a monochrome collage by using different examples of lettering. Cut or tear single letters or blocks of newsprint into shapes, contrasting light and dark tones.

Gluing Paper

Most water-based glues are ideal for paper, but some thin papers will crinkle and distort if the glue is too wet. Test the glue first on scrap paper to make sure it is suitable. For very fine paper and tissue, use a glue stick.

Paper Mosaic Collage

Patterns and Colors

An assortment of patterns and colors cut from printed paper makes an interesting mosaic picture. Figure out your mosaic design first on a suitable background. Cut the colored papers into small tile shapes. Arrange them according to your design, before sticking them down firmly.

Illustrations

Make a collection of pictures from magazines and brochures that relate to a particular theme, such as circular shapes. Mount them as a collage, choosing a background material that complements the picture. Raise some of the images on cardboard supports to give a 3-D effect.

Collage of Round Images

9

Collage in the Round

3-D Art from Paper

Picasso is well-known for his work both as a painter and a sculptor. He was the first major artist to use found objects in his artwork. Picasso's unique style of creating portraits can be seen in his three-dimensional sculpted heads, especially those made from cardboard and collage materials. Paper can be used in many different ways. Because paper is a flexible, fibrous material, it can be cut, coiled, or folded into a variety of 3-D shapes.

Coiling Paper

To make a coiled paper sculpture, you will need to find, or make, a shallow box to contain the paper coils. Then make pattern divisions in the box from strips of cardboard and glue them into place. Coil strips of paper of different colors and thicknesses. Position the coils in the box to create a pattern with them. By coiling strips of differing widths, you can also create a three-dimensional effect.

Coil strips of paper to make paper towers.

Wide strips make tall coils.

Narrow strips make small coils.

Place the coils inside a box to make a pattern.

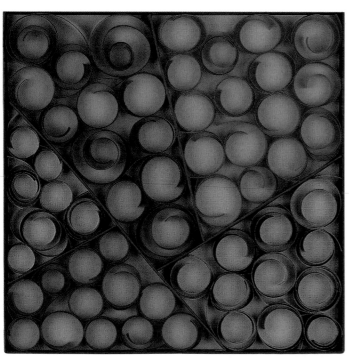

Coiled Paper Collage (from above)

Coiled Paper Collage (from the inside)

Paper Sculptures

When making a three-dimensional paper sculpture, you must first select stiff paper or cardboard. The separate pieces will be slotted together and the finished sculpture must be strong enough to support itself. You can glue several sheets of paper together to achieve the necessary stiffness.

Sketches of the Head

Paper Portraits

To make a 3-D portrait, you must first make sketches of a head both in profile and full-face. Sketch someone you know or make an imaginary portrait. Consider all aspects of the head — the face and features, plus the back of the head and neck. It may help you to look at some of Picasso's work. Keep the shapes simple.

Find suitable cardboard and work on the individual pieces separately. Cut out the shapes — the profiles, features, and slots — before adding any details. Finally, slot the pieces together when they are complete.

Make slots in the main pieces.

Paper Portraits

Picture Boxes

Collecting Printed Items

By now you will probably have gathered together lots of small printed items in your waste paper collection. Material such as labels, greeting cards, stamps, and stickers can be very colorful and interesting. Sort them according to color, pattern, or theme.

Collection of Printed Items

Decoupage

Decoupage is the art of decorating surfaces with paper cut outs. You can use your collection of small printed scraps to give a discarded box or container a brand new life.

Start with something simple to cover, like an old cardboard folder or wallet. Choose a selection of scraps that will cover the surfaces. Arrange them, moving them around until you are happy with the effect, and then glue them into place. Craft glue is ideal for sticking paper scraps to cardboard, but use it very sparingly.

Decorating the Folder

Fasten the folder by tying thread around cardboard circles secured with split-pins.

paper tassel

Decorated Boxes

Old boxes can be changed into useful storage containers, and gift boxes, by covering them with an assortment of attractive papers and scraps. Choose a sheet of used giftwrap or even an outdated road map. Do not forget to decorate the inside of your container with printed paper. Protect the decorated surfaces with a coat of watered-down glue.

Finishing Touches

If you are giving a decorated box to someone as a gift, cover it in materials that interest that person, for example, stamps, postcards, or sports pictures. Make matching handles, hinges, and fasteners for your box as shown here.

Decorated Boxes (above and below)

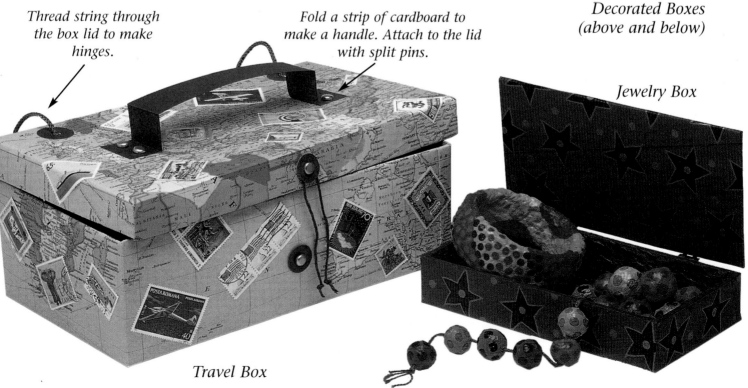

Thread string through the box lid to make hinges.

Fold a strip of cardboard to make a handle. Attach to the lid with split pins.

Jewelry Box

Travel Box

Paper Bags

Plastic Bags

Nowadays, millions of plastic bags are used daily for shopping. Plastic may be strong, but to dispose of plastic items is a major problem for a world with too much garbage. A single sheet of paper may tear easily, but layers of paper, glued together, can make a bag as strong as a plastic bag.

Plan for Bag

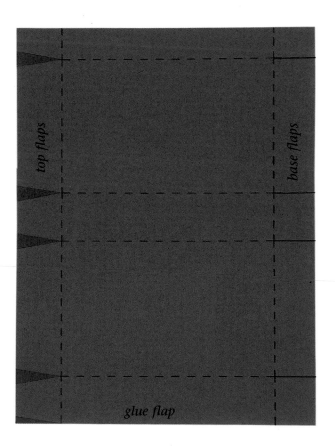

top flaps

base flaps

glue flap

Designing a Bag

The design for a bag must take into account a number of important considerations. The bag must be strong enough to take the weight of the contents. It also needs a strong, but comfortable, handle to make it user-friendly. Follow the diagram below measuring it to the size you would like. Remember a very deep bag may drag on the floor. Finally, the bag should look attractive. If you decide to make it out of layers of newspaper, paint the paper first.

Assembling the Bag

Fold top flaps.

Glue base flaps together.

Twisted Paper Handles

Extra Base

Folding and Gluing

Draw a plan first on a large sheet of scrap paper. Cut out the shape and crease along the fold lines. It may help to score the fold lines first if the paper is thick. Try to make the creases as sharp as possible. Assemble the bag, gluing down the flaps as shown. Place an extra cardboard base in the bag to reinforce the bottom.

Making the Handle

You can make a strong handle for the bag by twisting and gluing a long strip of newspaper into twine. Paint the handle to match the bag. Thread it through holes in the front and back of the bag. Pass it underneath for extra strength.

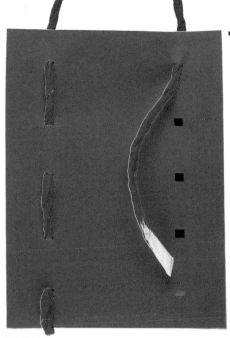

Threading the Handle

Gift Bags

You can also use discarded sheets of giftwrap or wallpaper. Decorate the bags with paint and colored paper scraps. Shredded newspaper is an ideal packing material to protect fragile presents.

Gift Bag Ideas

Use shredded paper for packing.

Recycled Cards

Recycling Cards

Sending greeting cards is traditional in many countries throughout the world. Cards are designed to fit every occasion. Some are printed on recycled paper, although many cards are not. Hundreds of thousands of trees are cut down every year to make paper to print cards. In developed countries, these come from managed forests and the industry is big business. You can help in a small way to reduce the amount of new paper that is produced by making new cards out of old cards.

Old Cards with New Backings

Lift the Flap Card

Zigzag Card

Collage Cards

New Cards from Old

Many cards are too attractive to throw away. Here are some ideas for reusing them. Cut out pictures from old cards and glue them to new backing cards. Make a lift-the-flap card by cutting flaps in a folded card and gluing pictures behind. Cut two pictures into strips and glue them alternately on a pleated card to make a zigzag card. Make collage cards by gluing several pictures onto a piece of folded cardboard.

Pop-Up Cards

Find a picture to use as a backing for a pop-up. Fold the backing picture in half, and measure a strip of cardboard half the width of the card. Attach the strip to the backing, as shown here. Glue a folded pop-up picture to the strip. You have a new pop-up card.

A Card Holder

Some cards are really too special to recycle because they are handmade or given by close family or friends. Here is an idea for making a card holder in which to keep them. Cut out the card holder shape from an old cereal box, as shown. Cover the box with a patchwork of cards, gluing them down firmly. Thread string through a small hole in the top of the holder to hang it up.

Glue ends of strip to background and glue the pop-up to the strip.

Pop-Up Cards

Use the top of the box to strengthen the base.

Cut line

Making the Card Holder

Patchwork Card Holder

Gift Cards and Tags

Masks and Disguises

Disguises

African peoples traditionally carved masks out of wood to represent protective spirits. They were worn during religious ceremonies. The ancient Greeks used masks in the theater.

All masks are a form of disguise. A disguise may be required for a costume party. For this, a half mask might be appropriate. It may be worn during a celebration such as Halloween, where the aim is to frighten. For this, a whole face mask would be more suitable.

Paper Disguises

All the paper disguises shown here are simple to make and fun to wear. Look through magazines for life-size photos of mouths, ears, and eyes. Cut out as many examples as you can find. Include items of clothing, like hats; and also include jewelry and sunglasses.

All the cut-outs should be glued on a piece of cardboard to strengthen them. Keep single features separate, or make a large face by gluing several together. Finally, attach each paper disguise to a stick to hold in front of your face.

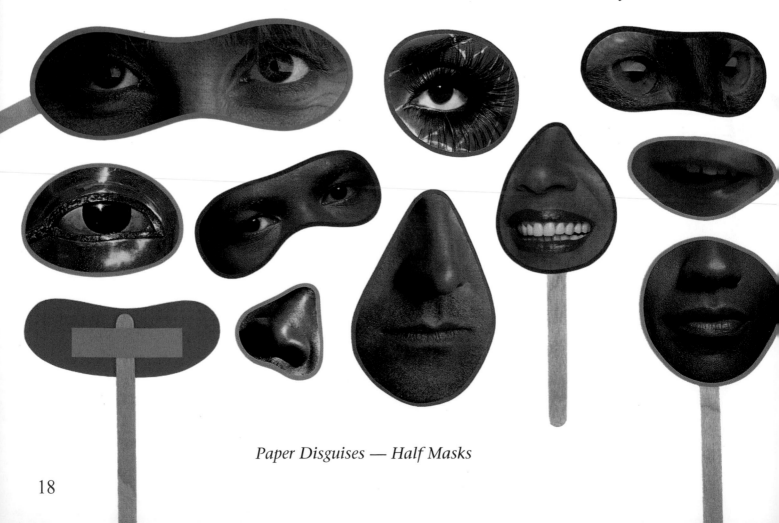

Paper Disguises — Half Masks

3-D Masks

These large paper masks are made to cover the whole head. They are made from a cylinder of paper that sits on the shoulders. First, you will need to make a paper cylinder that fits over your head comfortably.

Tape or paper clip the cylinder together temporarily, and ask a friend to carefully mark the eye and mouth holes with a pencil. Undo the cylinder and cut out the holes with scissors. Roll the mask back into shape and hold it together with strong tape.

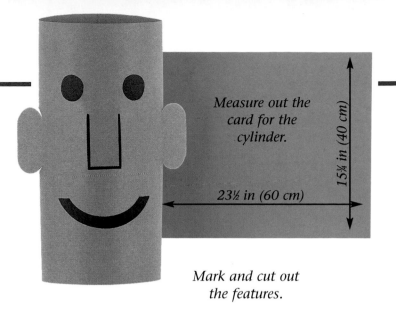

Measure out the card for the cylinder.

15¾ in (40 cm)

23½ in (60 cm)

Mark and cut out the features.

Basic 3-D Mask

Decorating the Mask

You can add features, such as hair, plumes, or feathers to the mask by cutting and folding them from scrap paper. Paint the mask with poster paints. Or, use magazine cut-outs for the features.

Examples of Finished Masks

Add features using paper curls, pleats, and frills.

19

Stuffed Shapes

Making Paper

Paper is made from the wood of spruces and firs, which are the fastest growing conifers. Much water is needed to turn timber into wood pulp, so pulp mills are usually beside rivers. River pollution can result from the dirty water leaving a pulp mill, and also from the chemical dioxin made during the bleaching of paper.

Stuffing Shapes

Clean waste paper can be saved and used. It is ideal as a stuffing material, because it can be crumpled into balls. Sheets of newspaper glued together make a strong fabric to hold the stuffing.

A Paper Mountain

At the beginning of the twentieth century, schoolchildren wrote on slates. Workbooks did not exist. People used cotton handkerchiefs, not paper tissues. Today, disposable paper products create a mountain of paper garbage. In the developed countries, each person uses about 265 lb (120 kg) of paper a year.

The waste newspaper in the United States in one year is equal to 30 million trees. Recycling saves trees. Items like egg cartons are now made from recycled paper.

Making The Basic Shape To Be Stuffed

Leave opening for stuffing.

Tear paper into small squares.

Attach together by gluing, stapling, or sewing.

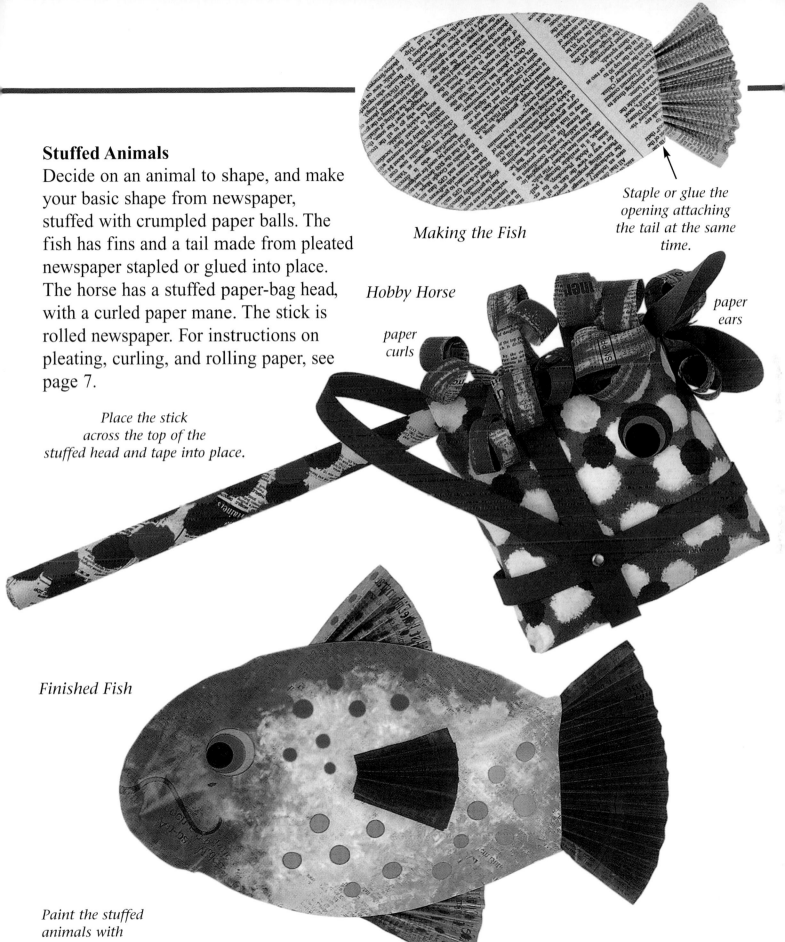

Stuffed Animals

Decide on an animal to shape, and make your basic shape from newspaper, stuffed with crumpled paper balls. The fish has fins and a tail made from pleated newspaper stapled or glued into place. The horse has a stuffed paper-bag head, with a curled paper mane. The stick is rolled newspaper. For instructions on pleating, curling, and rolling paper, see page 7.

Place the stick across the top of the stuffed head and tape into place.

Making the Fish

Staple or glue the opening attaching the tail at the same time.

Hobby Horse

paper curls

paper ears

Finished Fish

Paint the stuffed animals with poster paints.

21

Bracelets, Beads, Bowls

Papier-Mâché

Paper combined with liquid paste produces a strong material called papier-mâché. The liquid paste fills the holes in the surface of the paper to form a bond that sets hard.

Articles made from papier-mâché date back to the invention of paper in the second century A.D. The Chinese used papier-mâché to make masks for their warriors, because it was both lightweight and strong. In the seventeenth century, papier-mâché boxes and toys were hardened with lacquer (a shiny coating).

Papier-mâché items were imported into Europe from Eastern Asia. Since it was popular it could be used for many things, factories in Russia, Europe, and the U.S. produced a fantastic range of papier-mâché, from small boxes to furniture. It has also been used to build a boat, a Norwegian church, and a complete village in Australia.

There are two ways of making papier-mâché — by "layering" paper strips and glue over a mold, and by "pulping" paper. The second method is ideal for molding small shapes, such as jewelry.

Forming beads over a knitting needle

Making Paper Pulp Jewelry

Paint beads with poster paints and thread on a cord.

Forming the pulp around a cardboard roll.

Painted Bracelets

Paper Pulp Jewelry

To make paper pulp, fill a large bowl with small pieces of torn newspaper. Cover the paper with warm water and leave to soak overnight. Strain the water and add craft glue, mashing the pulp until it feels like soft clay. Mold the pulp over a greased knitting needle to make beads. The bracelets are shaped around empty tape rolls.

Papier-Mâché Bowls

You can make papier-mâché bowls and plates by using plastic bowls and plates as molds. First, smear the plastic mold with a thin coat of cooking oil, then cover with plastic wrap.

Start building up paper layers, gluing with watered-down craft glue. You can use strips of newspaper, but experiment with other colored scrap paper. Try using torn pieces of tissue and crêpe paper, gift wrap, and paper napkins.

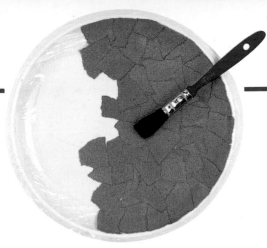

Adding Layers of Paper

Building Layers

You will need to build up at least six layers of papier-mâché to make a firm shape, more if you are using a fine paper like tissue. It helps to use a different colored paper for each layer. Leave to dry for several days before removing the mold. Either trim the rim and bind it with paper strips to make a neat edge, or leave it uneven. Bowls made from colored scrap papers do not need painting.

Papier-Mâché Plate and Bowl

23

Handmade Paper

Recycling Paper

Recycling weakens and shortens the cellulose fibers in paper. Consequently, there is a limit to the number of times that you can keep on recycling it to make more paper.

In France, scientists have discovered how to store paper indefinitely by turning it into small, dry pellets, which are used to make building blocks. In India, stationery is handmade from recycled cotton rags. The paper is often decorated with pressed flowers and grasses, and is usually exported to other countries.

Waste Paper

There are many different kinds of waste paper, which work for recycling. Newspapers are common, but the pulp discolors because of the printing ink. For making handmade papers, try to find a better quality paper, such as discarded computer or photocopier paper.

Basic Equipment

You will need a papermaking frame, like the one shown here. Ask an adult to help you make one. It consists of two wooden frames of equal size. The top frame, or *deckle*, rests on top of the bottom frame, or mold. The mold is covered with a fine mesh or cheesecloth.

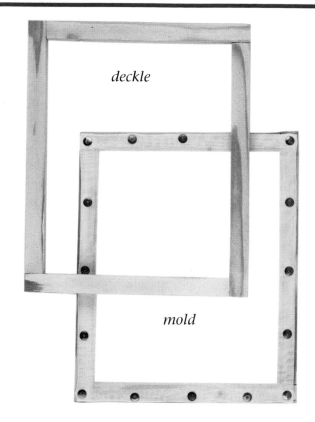

deckle

mold

Papermaking Frame

wood shavings

fresh and dried herbs

Materials for Papermaking

tea leaves and tea bags

How to Make Handmade Paper

Tear up the waste paper, cover with warm water, and leave to soak overnight. Squeeze out handfuls of the soaked paper, put them into a bowl, and cover with fresh water. Mash to a smooth pulp using your hands or a potato masher. At this stage, you can add any textured materials to the pulp.

Slide the mold into the pulp with the deckle on top. Shake it gently to spread the pulp evenly over the cheesecloth. Lift out and leave to drain. Remove the deckle, and turn the mold over carefully onto an absorbent cloth. Press the cheesecloth with an old sponge to remove as much water as possible.

Lift the mold slowly, leaving your sheet of paper on the cloth. Lay another cloth on top of the paper, and then put an old newspaper on top. Repeat the process until all the pulp has been used.

Cover the floor with thick newspaper and place the pile of cloths and newspaper in the middle. Put a board on top and gently stand on it to squeeze as much water from the paper as possible. Then remove the board, and lay each separate cloth out to dry in a warm place. Peel the sheets of paper from each cloth while they are still damp, and leave them flat to dry completely.

Colored waste papers were used to make the colored papers (1-3). The textured papers had the following added: (4) potato peelings; (5) chopped leaves; (6) wood chippings; (7) dried parsley; (8) spinach; (9) tea leaves.

Making Books

The First Books

The first books became possible only with the development of the art of papermaking. Before then, sheets of parchment, made from animal hide, were bound together to make a type of ancient book and even earlier, the ancient Egyptians used papyrus to make scrolls.

Making a Book

To make a book with sewn pages and a strong bound cover, you need to follow three simple stages. First, you will need to sew the pages of the book, then make the cover, and finally, attach the pages inside.

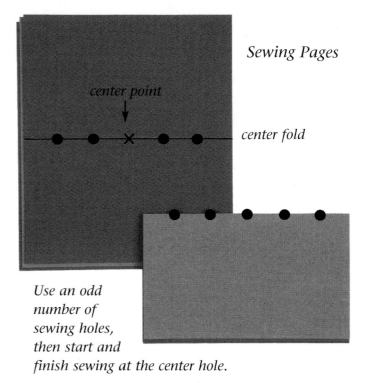

Sewing Pages

center point

center fold

Use an odd number of sewing holes, then start and finish sewing at the center hole.

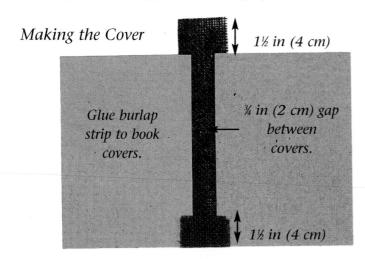

Making the Cover

1½ in (4 cm)

Glue burlap strip to book covers.

¾ in (2 cm) gap between covers.

1½ in (4 cm)

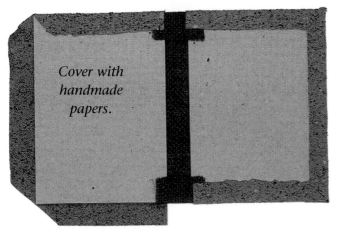

Cover with handmade papers.

Sewing pages

Decide how many pages your book will need, and cut your paper to size. Lay the sheets together and fold neatly in half. Open up and secure with paper clips before marking the center point on the crease with a small cross. Mark evenly spaced sewing holes on either side of the center cross. Pierce the holes with a thumb tack before sewing the pages together, following the order shown in the diagram.

Making the Cover

Take two pieces of cardboard, slightly larger than your page size, and bind them together with burlap. Cut the burlap 4 in (10 cm) wide and 3 in (8 cm) longer than the cardboard and attach it as shown here. Cover the outside of the book with pieces of your handmade paper.

Attaching the Pages

To attach the sewn pages to the cover, glue the first page down inside the front cover and the last page inside the back cover. Take your time, and make sure the pages are straight.

Attaching Pages to Cover

Decorative Covers

We have used handmade papers to make the books shown here. The papers themselves are beautifully colored and textured, and make ideal decorative book covers.

Books Made Using Handmade Papers and Textured Covers

Embossing Designs

It is also possible to create embossed patterns on the papers to make attractive covers. Dampen the paper and gently push coiled string, wire mesh, or other raised images into the surface. Leave under a heavy weight until dry.

embossed design using chicken wire

embossed design using string

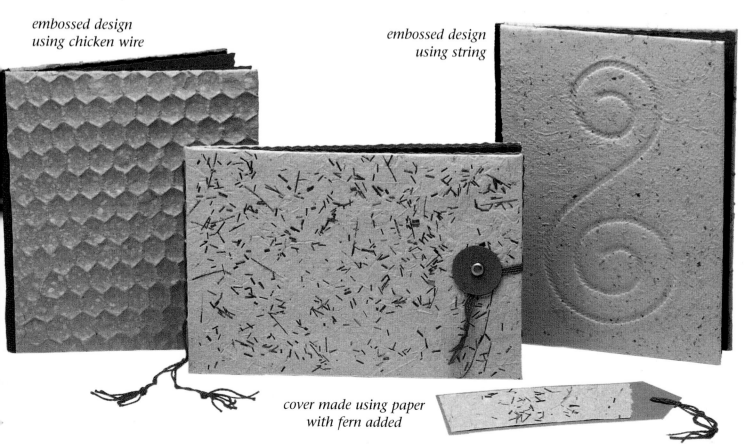

cover made using paper with fern added

27

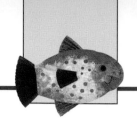

Collecting Scraps

Scrapbooks

By the end of the nineteenth century, many people in industrialized countries began to have more leisure time. Children were encouraged to spend their play time in useful ways. Collecting scraps became a popular leisure activity. Today, the term *scrapbook* has a much wider application. It can be used to display a collection of postcards, photographs, tickets, programs, labels, stamps, and other souvenirs.

Making a Scrapbook

Why not make a scrapbook to hold your collection? Use recycled materials or your handmade papers to make the book. Follow the instructions on page 24 to sew pages together. Use scrap cardboard for the covers, and decorate them with appropriate items. There are many ways of arranging a collection. Some things can be stuck directly on the pages. You could attach small, transparent bags to your pages and slip items inside. They can then be moved around if necessary.

Scrapbooks

Mix and Match Book

Cut out cartoon pictures from old greeting cards to make this amusing book. Follow the instructions on page 26. Cut across the pages, leaving a ⅓-in (1 cm) space uncut on either side of the center fold. Now stick the cut-out pictures on the pages. Have fun making some strange people.

Storing Records

You can make a useful storage box in which to keep a photograph or postcard collection. Use the bottom of an old shoe box for the main drawer, and make an outer cover from scrap cardboard. Decorate the outside of the box. Make a series of blank record cards to slot in between the items in your collection, so you can organize them in order of subject or date.

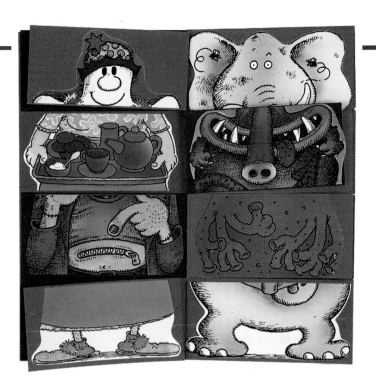

Mix and Match Book

Making the Record Box

glue

scrap cardboard

shoe box

Box for Postcard Collection

Decorate the box with a postcard collage.

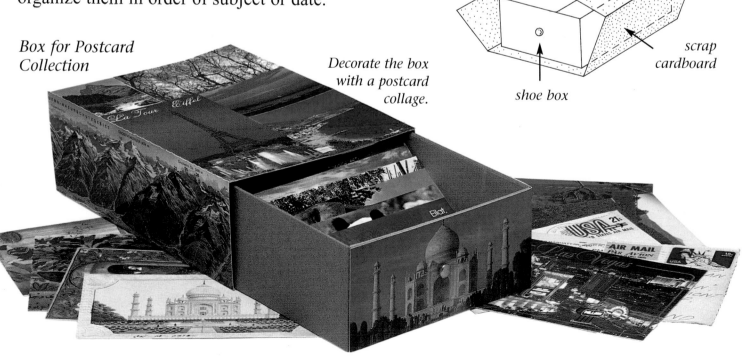

Glossary

burlap A strong, coarse fabric made from jute and used to make sacks.

codex (plural: codices) A volume of manuscripts of ancient text.

conifers Trees or shrubs bearing cones and evergreen leaves. The group includes pines, spruces, firs, and larches.

decoupage The decoration of a surface with cut-out shapes or illustrations.

developed countries Highly industrialized countries, such as those in Europe and North America; also Japan and Australia.

developing countries Countries that rely on agriculture but are becoming more industrialized, such as most African, Asian, and South American countries.

dioxin Any of various chemical by-products resulting from the manufacture of certain herbicides and bactericides.

ecosystem The interaction between a community and its nonliving environment.

embossed A surface with a raised decoration in low relief.

flax A plant with blue flowers. The fibrous stems are used to make linen thread.

hardwood Close-grain wood from deciduous trees.

jute A tropical plant.

lacquer A hard, shiny coating or varnish often used to protect furniture.

landfill sites Low-lying dumps filled up with layers of garbage and earth.

lignin A part of the cell walls of certain plants, making the plant stiff.

memorabilia Important items from the past.

methane A gas that can be burned and used as fuel.

monochrome Black and white artwork.

opaque Refers to a material that does not transmit light.

papyrus Paper made by the ancient Egyptians from the stems of an aquatic plant.

parchment Durable manuscript material made from treated animal skin.

profile A side view of the head.

snuff box A small box for snuff (powdered tobacco).

softwood Open-grained wood from conifers.

toxic fumes Poisonous fumes.

translucent Semitransparent, allowing the passage of a certain amount of light.

For More Information

Books to Read

Artistry in Paper, Paul Jackson (Kodansha, 2006)

Collage (Step-by-Step), Judy Balchin (Heinemann Library, 2003)

Earth-Friendly Crafts for Kids (50 Awesome Things to Make with Recycled Stuff), Joe Rhatigan and Heather Smith (Lark Books, 2002)

Making Magic Windows (Creating Cut-Paper Art), Carmen Lomas Garza (Children's Book Press, 1999)

Nature's Art Box, Laura C. Martin (Storey Publishing, 2003)

Paper Punch Art, Laura Torres (American Girl, 2001)

Papier Mache (Step-by-Step), Judy Balchin (Heinemann, 2000)

Recycled Crafts Box, Laura C. Martin (Storey Publishing, 2004)

The Kids Multi-Cultural Craft Book, Roberta Gould (Williamson Publishing Company, 2003)

Places to Visit

American Folk Art Museum,
45 West 53rd Street, New York NY 10019
(Historic and contemporary folk art, including sculpture and paintings)

American Visionary Art Museum,
800 Key Highway, Baltimore, Maryland 21230
(Displaying art from recycled materials including customized 'Art Cars', sculpture, and mosaics)

Boston Children's Museum,
300 Congress Street, Boston MA 02210
(Includes The Recycle Shop, a children's activity center where re-used materials can be transformed into art projects)

Metropolitan Museum of Art,
1000 Fifth Avenue. New York, New York 10028
(Wide range of exhibits, including jewelry, mosaics, sculpture, block printing, and textiles and dyeing)

The Noyes Museum,
Lily Lake Road, Oceanville, New Jersey 08231
(Collection of folk arts and crafts, including ceramics, jewelry, paper and print, and wood)

The Museum of Printing History,
1324 West Clay Street, Houston, Texas 77019
(Runs workshops for children on papermaking and printmaking)

UCM Museum, 22275 Hwy 36,
Abita Springs, LA 70420, Ph: 985-892-2624
(Small, unusual collection of art made from recycled materials, mosaics, and more)

Web Sites

Due to the changing nature of Internet links, PowerKids Press has developed an online list of Web sites related to the subject of this book. This site is regularly updated. Please use this link to access this list:
www.powerkidslinks.com/everydayart/paper

Index